MW00901224

DATE D.

SAVING THE MANATEE

by Karen Latchana Kenney

Ideas for Parents and Teachers

Pogo Books let children practice reading informational text while introducing them to nonfiction features such as headings, labels, sidebars, maps, and diagrams, as well as a table of contents, glossary, and index.

Carefully leveled text with a strong photo match offers early fluent readers the support they need to succeed.

Before Reading

- "Walk" through the book and point out the various nonfiction features. Ask the student what purpose each feature serves.
- Look at the glossary together. Read and discuss the words.

Read the Book

- Have the child read the book independently.
- Invite him or her to list questions that arise from reading.

After Reading

- Discuss the child's questions. Talk about how he or she might find answers to those questions.
- Prompt the child to think more. Ask: What did you know about manatees before reading this book? What more would you like to learn about them?

Pogo Books are published by Jump!
5357 Penn Avenue South
Minneapolis, MN 55419
www.jumplibrary.com

Library of Congress Cataloging-in-Publication Data

Names: Kenney, Karen Latchana, author.
Title: Saving the manatee / by Karen Latchana Kenney.
Description: Pogo books edition. | Minneapolis, MN : Jump!, Inc., [2019]
Series: Great animal comebacks
Audience: Age 7-10. | Includes index.
Identifiers: LCCN 2018036949 (print)
LCCN 2018039025 (ebook)
ISBN 9781641282895 (ebook)
ISBN 9781641282888 (hardcover : alk. paper)
Subjects: LCSH: Manatees–Conservation–Juvenile literature.
Classification: LCC QL737.S63 (ebook)
LCC QL737.S63 K46 2019 (print) | DDC 599.55–dc23
LC record available at https://lccn.loc.gov/20180369492

Editor: Jenna Trnka
Designer: Anna Peterson

Photo Credits: 33Karen33/iStock, cover, 10; Eric Baccega/Age Fotostock, 1, 20-21; Wayne Lynch/Age Fotostock, 3, 6-7; Morales/Age Fotostock, 4; Getty, 5; National Geographic Image Collection/Alamy, 8-9; Brian J. Skerry/Getty, 11; Alex Couto/Shutterstock, 12-13; Paul Nicklen/Getty, 14-15; Wolfgang Poelzer/SeaPics.com/Alamy, 16-17; mixmotive/iStock, 18; imageBROKER/Alamy, 19; Norbert Probst/Getty, 23.

Printed in the United States of America at Corporate Graphics in North Mankato, Minnesota.

TABLE OF CONTENTS

CHAPTER 1

LOSING THE MANATEE

A manatee floats. It is near the bottom of Crystal River in Florida. Why? Food grows here.

snout

It pulls plants toward its mouth with its snout. West Indian manatees have grazed on plants here for centuries. But they were once **endangered**.

Native American tribes first hunted manatees for food. Then European settlers started hunting them in the 1500s. These large **mammals** swim slowly. They live in shallow water. And they come to the surface for air. So they are easy to catch. Many were hunted.

DID YOU KNOW?

Manatees live in warm water. Why? Cold water can kill them. They do not have **blubber** to keep them warm.

There are three kinds of manatees. West Indian manatees live by Florida. Amazonian manatees live in the Amazon River in South America. West African manatees live in rivers in Africa.

TAKE A LOOK!

West Indian manatees once lived in all of the Gulf of Mexico. They lived along more of the U.S. East Coast. They also lived farther down the coast of South America. Take a look at where they live now.

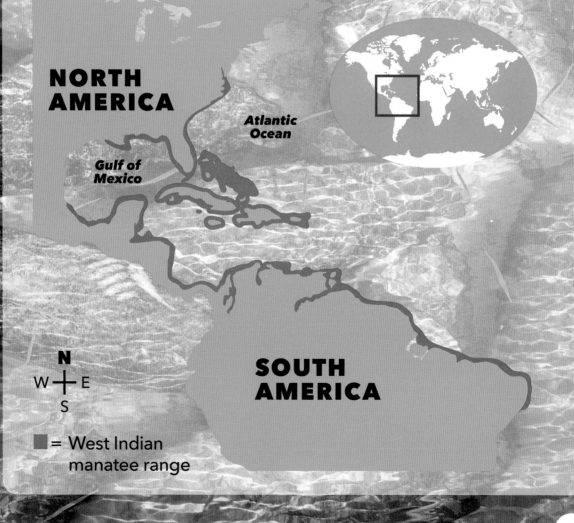

NORTH AMERICA

Atlantic Ocean

Gulf of Mexico

SOUTH AMERICA

N
W + E
S

■ = West Indian manatee range

CHAPTER 2

SAVING THE
MANATEE

Manatees were hard to find by the late 1800s. Florida passed a law in 1893. People needed a **permit** to hunt or catch manatees. Starting in 1907, hunters without permits paid a fine. Or they went to jail.

propeller

This helped manatees.
Their **populations** grew.
But there was a new threat.
Powerboats. Boat **propellers**
hit and killed many manatees.

In the 1970s, scientists started counting manatees. How? From above, in airplanes. They found that just a few hundred were left. Laws passed in 1972 and 1973. One was the Endangered **Species** Act (ESA). Now no one could hunt manatees.

radio tag

But people were taking over their **habitats**. They were building near the water. Their boats were harming manatees. Florida passed another law. It made it illegal to touch or disturb manatees. Why? They scare easily. Touching them can make them move to cold areas.

The U.S. government made a plan. To do what? Better study manatees. Scientists counted their populations again. They used **radio tags** to track them, too.

Then the U.S. government made a **refuge** for them. It is the Crystal River National Wildlife Refuge in Florida. People can watch manatees. But they cannot disturb them.

DID YOU KNOW?

Manatees are a **keystone species**. They are important to their habitat. Why? They help keep it in balance. Their behaviors tell scientists if their habitat is changing.

MANATEE VIEWING PROHIBITIONS

THE FOLLOWING ACTIVITIES ARE PROHIBITED
WHILE VIEWING MANATEES IN KINGS BAY

NO
- CHASING/PURSUING
- CORNERING/SURROUNDING
- POKING/PRODDING/STABBING
- FEEDING/WATERING
- RIDING/HOLDING
- GRABBING/PINCHING/STANDING-ON

DO NOT
- DISTURB/TOUCH A RESTING OR FEEDING MANATEE
- DIVE DOWN ON A RESTING OR FEEDING MANATEE
- SEPARATE MANATEES FROM A GROUP; INCLUDING MOTHER FROM CALF
- ACTIVELY INITIATE CONTACT WITH A TAGGED MANATEE OR ASSOCIATED GEAR
- ENTER MANATEE SANCTUARIES (PERSONS OR EQUIPMENT)
- INTERFERE WITH MANATEE RESCUE/RESEARCH ACTIVITIES

50CFR17.104(b)

CHAPTER 3

MORE MANATEES

Florida also made manatee zones. Boaters have to slow down in these water areas.

MANATEE ZONE

SLOW SPEED
MINIMUM WAKE

Manatees still get hurt. But zoos and other places help. They rescue hurt manatees. They help them heal. Then they release them into the wild.

calf

With laws and our help, manatee numbers are up. They were taken off the endangered list. But they are still **threatened**.

Boats still hurt them. They still get tangled in fishing nets. And they are still losing their habitat. But with our help, these gentle giants can continue to graze in Florida's waters. How will you help?

ACTIVITIES & TOOLS

SWIM WITH MANATEES

Do you want to swim with manatees? In the wild, this disturbs them. But you can try it online!

What You Need:
- computer
- notebook
- pen

1 **Ask an adult to help you visit this website on a computer:**
https://www.friendsofcrystalriver.org/tour/ThreeSistersSprings.html

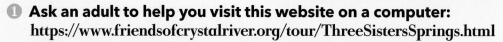

2 **Explore the Crystal River National Wildlife Refuge online. Write down notes. What do the manatees look like? What do you see underwater?**

3 **Write a paragraph about what you saw. Did you learn anything new about manatees and their habitat?**

blubber: The layer of fat under the skin of a whale or other large marine mammal.

calf: A young manatee.

endangered: In danger of becoming extinct.

habitats: The places and natural conditions in which animals or plants live.

keystone species: A species of plant or animal that has a major impact on and is essential to the ecosystem in which it belongs.

mammals: Warm-blooded animals that give birth to live young.

permit: An official document that gives someone permission to do something.

populations: The total numbers of living things in certain areas.

propellers: Sets of rotating blades that provide force to move objects through the water or air.

radio tags: Devices placed on animals that send radio signals out to scientists, who use them to track the animals.

refuge: A protected place where hunting is not allowed and animals can live and breed safely.

species: One of the groups into which similar animals and plants are divided.

threatened: Likely to become an endangered species.

INDEX

TO LEARN MORE

Finding more information is as easy as 1, 2, 3.

1. Go to www.factsurfer.com
2. Enter "savingthemanatee" into the search box.
3. Click the "Surf" button to see a list of websites.